*"The diversity in the human family
should be the cause of love and harmony,
as it is in music where many different notes
blend together in the making of a perfect chord."*

Abdú'l-Bahá

The Persian Alphabet

We want to simplify your Persian learning journey as it is such a unique & enigmatic language. There are 32 official Persian letters. The letters change form depending on their position in a word or when they appear separate from other letters. For example, the letter g<u>h</u>ayn غ has four ways of being written depending on where it appears in any given word:

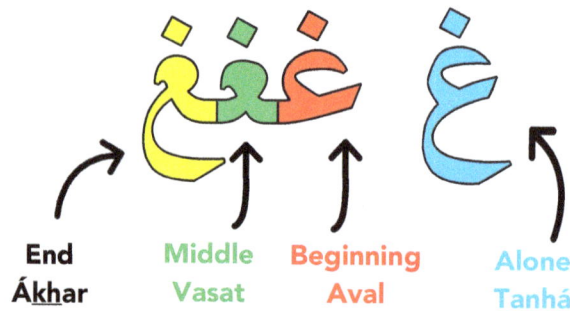

غغغ غغ غ

End	Middle	Beginning	Alone
Á<u>kh</u>ar	Vasat	Aval	Tanhá

It is important to note that Persian books are read from right to left (←). There are 7 separate/stand-alone letters that do not connect in the same way to adjacent letters (these will be depicted in blue). They are:

Stand alone
Tanhá vámístan

ا د ذ ر ز ژ و

The short vowels a, e & o are usually omitted in literature and are depicted by markings above & below letters (ـــِـ). They are not allocated a letter name, unlike their long vowel counterparts á: alef, í: ye & ú: váv (و ی آ).

Englisi	Farsi	Englisi	Farsi	Englisi	Farsi
A a	اَ اً اً	M m	م مـمـم mím	Y y	ی یـیـی ye
Á á	آ ا ا 'alef	N n	ن نـنـن nún	Z z	ذ نذ zál
B b	ب بـیـب Be	O o	اُ اُ اُ	Z z	ز زز ze
D d	د دد dál	P p	پ پـیـپ pe	Z z	ض ضـضـض zád
E e	اِ ٍٍ 	Q q	ق قـقـق qáf	Z z	ظ ظـظـظ zá
F f	ف فـفـف fe	R r	ر رر re	**Ch** ch	چ چـچـچ che
G g	گ گـگـگ gáf	S s	س سـسـس sin	**Gh** gh	غ غـغـغ ghayn
H h	ه هـهـه he	S s	ص صـصـص sád	**Kh** kh	خ خـخـخ khe
H h	ح حـحـح he	S s	ث ثـثـث se	**Sh** sh	ش شـشـش shín
Í í	ی یـیـی ye	T t	ت تـتـت te	**Zh** zh	ژ ژژ zhe
J j	ج جـجـج jim	T t	ط طـطـط tá	**'**	ع عـعـع ayn
K k	ک کـکـک káf	Ú ú	و وو váv		
L l	ل لـلـل lám	V v	و وو váv		

Letter Guide©

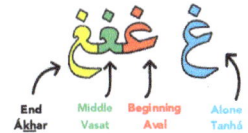

End
Ákhar   Middle
Vasat   Beginning
Avai   Alone
Tanhá

Pronunciation Guide©

Persian	English	Pronunciation
اَ	a	**a**nt
آ	á	**a**rm
ب	b	**b**at
د	d	**d**og
اِ	e	**e**nd
ف	f	**f**un
گ	g	**g**o
ه	h	**h**at
ح	h	**h**at
ی	í	m**ee**t
ج	j	**j**et
ک	k	**k**ey
ل	l	**l**ove
م	m	**m**e
ن	n	**n**ap
اُ	o	**o**n
پ	p	**p**at
ق	q/gh*	me**r**ci
ر	r	**r**un
س	s	**s**un
ص	s	**s**un
ث	s	**s**un

Persian	English	Pronunciation
ت	t	**t**op
ط	t	**t**op
و	ú	m**oo**n
و	v	**v**an
ی	y	**y**es
ذ	z	**z**oo
ز	z	**z**oo
ض	z	**z**oo
ظ	z	**z**oo
چ	**ch**	**ch**air
غ	**gh***	me**r**ci
خ	**kh***	ba**ch**
ش	**sh**	**sh**are
ژ	**zh**	plea**s**ure
ع	'	uh-oh†

*	: guttural sound from back of throat
†	: glottal stop, breathing pause
ّ	: Indicates a double letter
ً	: Indicates the letter n sound
لا	: Indicates combination of letter l & á (lá)
ای	: Indicates the long í sound (ee in m**ee**t)
اِی	: Indicates the long í sound (ee in m**ee**t)
(...)	: Indicates colloquial use

piano

píáno

پیانو

í: as (ee) in m<u>ee</u>t
á: as (a) in <u>a</u>rm

violin

víolen

ويولِن

í: as (ee) in m<u>ee</u>t

Persian frame drum

daf
دَف

drum

tabl

طَبل

[Persian goblet drum: tonbak]

maracas

<u>kh</u>á<u>sh</u> <u>kh</u>á<u>sh</u>ak

خاش خاشَک

á: as (a) in <u>a</u>rm

castanet

gháshoghak

قَاشُثَق

á: as (a) in arm

trombone

trúmbún

ترومبون

ú: as (oo) in m<u>oo</u>n

[trumpet: <u>sh</u>ípúr]

saxophone

sáksífon

ساكسيفون

á: as (a) in <u>a</u>rm
í: as (ee) in m<u>ee</u>t

flute

folút

فُلوت

ú: as (oo) in m<u>oo</u>n

recorder

folúte ríkorder

فُلوتِ ریکوردِر

ú: as (oo) in m<u>oo</u>n
í: as (ee) in m<u>ee</u>t

harp

chang

چَنگ

guitar

gítár

گیتار

í: as (ee) in m<u>ee</u>t
á: as (a) in <u>a</u>rm

[Persian guitar: setár]
[Electric guitar: gítare elektrík]

dulcimer

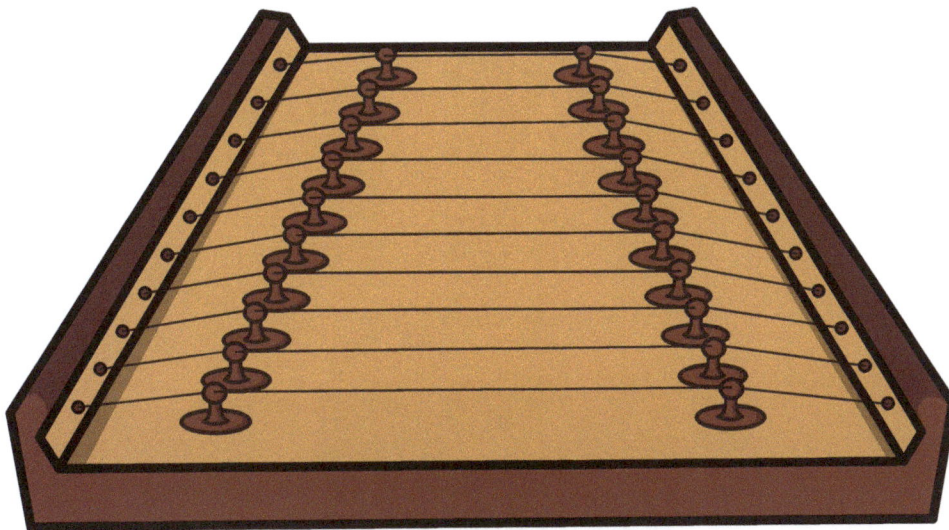

santúr

سَنتور

ú: as (oo) in m<u>oo</u>n

bass

bás

باس

á: as (a) in arm

ukelele

yúkeleleh

يو كِلله

ú: as (oo) in m<u>oo</u>n

tamborine

dáyereh zangí

داﻳِﺮﻩ زَنگی

á: as (a) in <u>a</u>rm
í: as (ee) in m<u>ee</u>t

triangle

sáze mosallas

سازِ مُثَلَّث

á: as (a) in arm

xylophone

zílofon

زيلوفون

í: as (ee) in meet

cymbals

senjehá

سِنجِها

harmonica

sázdahaní

ساز دَهَنی

á: as (a) in <u>a</u>rm
í: as (ee) in m<u>ee</u>t

whistle

sút zadan

سوت زَدَن

ú: as (oo) in m<u>oo</u>n

[Persian finger snap: be<u>sh</u>kan]

singing

áváz <u>kh</u>ándan

آواز خواندَن

á: as (a) in <u>a</u>rm

Quick Reference: Musical Instruments

English	Finglisi™	Persian
piano	píano	پیانو
violin	víolen	ویولن
drum	tabl	طَبل
goblet drum	tombak	تُمبَک
handheld frame drum	daf	دَف
maracas	khásh kháshak	خاش خاشَک
castanet	gháshoghak	قاشُقَک
trumpet	shípúr	شیپور
trombone	trúmbún	ترومبون
saxophone	sáksífon	ساکسیفون
flute	folút	فُلوت
recorder	folúte ríkorder	فُلوتِ ریکوردِر
harp	chang	چَنگ
guitar	gítar	گیتار
Persian guitar	setár	سِتار
electric guitar	gítare elektrík	گیتارِ اِلِکتریک

Quick Reference: Musical Instruments

English	Finglisi™	Persian
dulcimer	santúr	سَنتور
bass	bás	باس
ukelele	yúkeleleh	یوکِللِه
tamborine	dáyereh zangí	تَنبور
triangle	sáze mosallas	سازِ مُثَلَث
xylophone	zílofon	زیلوفون
bell	zang	زَنگ
cymbals	senjeha	سِنجِها
harmonica	sázdahaní	سازدَهَنی
whistle	sút zadan	سوت زَدَن
dancing	raghsídan	رَقصیدَن
singing	áváz khúndan	آواز خواندن
English	Englísí	اِنگلیسی
Persian	Fársí	فارسی

www.ingramcontent.com/pod-product-compliance
Lightning Source LLC
Chambersburg PA
CBHW040245100426

42811CB00011B/1152